What people

'Thanks for you feel so blessed and hap

'Your wisdom, intuition, straightness and guidance never leaves me.'

'Thank you for your constant support, guidance and wisdom. I have come so far from where I was with your sessions. I feel the most confident version of myself. I am still doing the valuing exercise and it is getting easier and easier everyday.'

'I really appreciate all the help and support you gave me, and the strength and courage to carry on and take each day at a time.'

'You were a great comfort to me.'

Thank you so much for your patience and mostly your understanding in helping me to come to terms and understand myself.'

'Your intuition and honesty have touched me.'

'Thank you for all your kind help and calming influence over the last couple of years.'

'I have really gained such a lot from our sessions and feel so much more positive and ready to move on.'

'Following on from my counseling sessions with you I have made great progress. Why did I wait 60 years to get help?'

'I want to express my gratitude for all the help, support and encouragement you gave which was instrumental in enabling me achieve success. You gave me the incentive and courage to carry on.'

'My first appointment with Anne was at a point in my life when I was at a very low ebb due to the pressures caused by major changes at work. Through her professional and supportive counseling, I was able to deal with the changes and I now feel much more positive.'

Value You

7 Steps to Overcome Low Self-Esteem and Low Self-Worth to Achieve Amazing Personal Change

ANNE GROOM

First Printing: 2020

Copyright © 2020 by Anne Groom

All rights reserved.

Printed in the United Kingdom.

This book or any of its parts may not be reproduced or used in any manner whatsoever without the express written permission of the author and publisher. However, brief quotations in a book review or scholarly journal are permitted.

Authors and their publications mentioned in this work and bibliography have their copyright protection.

The author is unassociated with any product or vendor in this book.

"Search For The Hero" lyrics © Sony BMG

Contents

Free gift! 11

Acknowledgments 13

About the author 15

Who will benefit from reading this book? 17

How to use this book 19

1 Value yourself – An exercise that will change your life 21

    The Valuing Exercise 25

    I love and appreciate myself 28

        A client story 1 – Nathan 32

    Valuing yourself in the workplace 34

        A client story 2 – Jane 37

    Summary 39

2 Recognize your daily achievements 41
Summary 49

3 Keep a personal journal – Delight in your progress 51
How do you feel doing the Valuing Exercise? 54
Affirmations 55
Benefits of journaling 56
Summary 59

4 Listen to your self-talk: the chatter inside your head 61
The power of positivity 67
Developing a positive attitude 68
Summary 69

5 Find the hero inside yourself: Value and recognize your self-worth 71
Confidence boost 77
More tips to help you feel great about yourself 80

Summary 82

6 Be kind to yourself and build your self-esteem 83

How can you be kinder to yourself? 86

Building your self-esteem 89

Summary 90

7 Get to 'I'm OK and you're OK': Bringing it all together 91

Appendix 1: Client comments on the Valuing Exercise 99

Appendix 2: Valuing Exercise form 101

Remember your free gift 103

One final thing... 107

Index 109

Free gift!

As a "thank you" for obtaining this book, I'd like to give you a free gift: a PDF called *Simple Breathing and Calming Method*. It's worth its weight in gold.

Here's the link: www.selfhealsystems.com/free

I hope that you find this helpful.

Acknowledgments

Thank you to my husband Ron and sons Philip, Michael, David and Andrew for their love and support, throughout my counseling career.

Thank you also to:

My friends Myra and Joyce for their continued encouragement.

Christopher John Payne, my coach and mentor, whose consistent support and expertise was invaluable.

Naomi Munts for efficiently sorting out my difficulties with the book template.

Mohamed Mustafa for designing the cover for this book, and Yuliia Nikolaieva for the illustrations.

Andrew Groom for the diagrams.

Michael and Shelley Groom for proof-reading and editing.

Darren Boyd-Annells who, in the latter stages of writing, helped keep my momentum going.

The clients I have worked with over the years who, each in their own way, have unknowingly inspired me to write this book.

About the author

Anne Groom trained as a teacher and taught for several years in Colleges of Further Education. Whilst teaching, she trained to become a counselor and psychotherapist and, for more than 25 years, has been self-employed as a Counseling Psychotherapist and Trainer.

Anne Groom

She is a Humanistic Integrative Psychotherapist including Person Centred Counseling, Transactional Analysis and Cognitive Behavioural Therapy (CBT) and other modalities. Anne has a wide range of experience working with people of all ages, with many different issues and difficulties. Anne draws on her training, experience and knowledge using a holistic approach in a way which is unique for each individual.

Who will benefit from reading this book?

Many people are aware of not feeling good about themselves, lacking in confidence and having a poor self-esteem.

If this applies to you it is not your fault, and the good thing is that you can do something about it.

As we progressed through childhood many of us were told by our well-meaning caregivers what **not** to do and what we **hadn't** done well, instead of being told what they **wanted** us to do and what we **had** done well.

You might have been judged by your behavior, instead of the the beautiful little child that you were. The scene is set for many children growing up to be unsure about their own character and abilities, resulting in poor self-esteem.

This book *'Value You'* will go a long way towards putting this right, resulting in you achieving amazing personal growth with much greater self-esteem and self-worth.

How to use this book

I encourage you to take your time as you work through the chapters in this book. It would be appropriate to read one chapter a day.

Rushing through the book will not be helpful. Pacing yourself and taking it more slowly will be most beneficial.

Trust the process of working on the concepts covered in this book.

You are entering a process which ultimately will enable you to feel better about yourself.

1

Value yourself – An exercise that will change your life

"You yourself, as much as anybody in the entire Universe, deserve your love and affection."

— *Buddha*

Perhaps you have been feeling depressed and/or suffering from anxiety. Both these conditions can be the result of a build up or accumulation of difficult life experiences, especially if they have happened over a short space of time. You may not have had the opportunity to talk about them to anyone, a trusted friend, health professional or counselor.

'Under-pinning these emotional and psychological issues is low self-esteem.'

During my years of counseling all my clients, many suffering from depression and/or anxiety, I have found that often under-pinning these emotional and psychological issues is low self-esteem and low self-worth.

Many people do not value themselves. When asked 'What do you do that shows that you value yourself?' they find it difficult to reply. Or they will tell me that they value themselves for being a good mother, father, husband or wife. This is what they do for others rather than what they do for themselves. They do not tell me things that they have done, that show that they value themselves. Perhaps this applies to you.

It can come to a point in the counseling process when the person's progress will be limited unless they begin to value themselves more. The low self-esteem and self-worth will hamper their breakthrough in terms of achieving what they set out to achieve. They may want to feel better and for the depression to lift, to feel calmer, to be more proactive in their own lives, and be more decisive. The person may wish to be more assertive in their relationships with their partners, husbands, wives, and other other people. Or it may be that they want to be more assertive with their work colleagues so that they are able to prevent and manage workplace stress.

> **Oxford Dictionary Definition**
>
> *Self-esteem* – a feeling of being happy with your own character and abilities.

The Valuing Exercise

During counseling I enable people to learn to value themselves and I would like to encourage you to do the same, to help you feel better about yourself, and overcome depression and anxiety. This involves you completing a simple written exercise each day.

It is a simple exercise and is not necessarily easy. More about that later.

What I want you to do is to buy or find a notebook you already have that you can dedicate to this exercise. Ideally it will be a notebook that is pleasant to use, the paper is of good quality and is easy to write on.

Hopefully it will be visually attractive and you will find it aesthetically pleasing to handle and use. You might already have something at home which will be suitable, or you may go shopping to look for a notebook and choose one that you like especially for this exercise. Some people choose a plain notebook which they then decorate themselves. This can be therapeutic in itself.

I want you to write down 3 things each day that you value yourself for. This is not about writing down and valuing what you do for others. This exercise is about what you do for yourself, to show that you are of value and that you are valuing yourself.

You write down and complete each sentence:

I value myself for ....

I value myself for ....

I value myself for ....

Please remember, this is about what you do for yourself, not what you do for others. Like many other people you may find this exercise slightly challenging to begin with. As I said a moment ago the exercise is simple, though perhaps not easy, and you will soon get the knack of doing it.

'Write down 3 things each day that you value yourself for.'

The apparently smallest thing that you value yourself for is relevant. It is too easy to disregard the smaller things that you do for yourself. Please include them. The benefits add up and the whole is greater than the sum of the parts. Each thing that you value yourself for is like the ripple effect from a small pebble in a large pool… far reaching. Here are some examples:

- Having a shower when you really don't feel like taking one.

- Making sure that you take your breaks at work instead of working through them.

- Buying yourself a bunch of flowers.
- Going out for a 30-minute walk.
- Speaking up for yourself.
- Saying 'no' when appropriate.
- Giving yourself a manicure.
- Buying yourself a magazine.
- Going to the gym.
- Buying healthy ingredients for a meal.

For me personally it might be making sure that I drink enough water, making sure that I don't skip meals, getting enough sleep or buying a pretty pot plant.

I love and appreciate myself

I have given you some examples of how you might value yourself and I want you to do this exercise every day.

Value Yourself

When you have written down the three things that you value yourself for, at some point during the day read them back to yourself. Take everything in and absorb.

Then write down:

And I love and appreciate myself.

Please see Appendix 2 for a pro former.

You might find this exercise quite tough to begin with, though you will soon get into it and get the hang of it.

You may find it difficult to find three things each day that you value yourself for so, to begin with, it is OK for you to repeat, i.e. write down twice, one of the things that you value yourself for.

It is also OK for you to write the same thing down two days running. After a few days of doing the exercise I'd expect you to be able to write down three different things that you value yourself for.

Committing yourself to doing the exercise may result in you doing something of value for yourself that you wouldn't otherwise do, if you weren't doing the exercise. I know that you might think that this is rather contrived and that somehow it doesn't count. I can assure you that it does count because, as you do this exercise, a part of you 'hears' you valuing yourself; that part where you are lacking in confidence, self-worth and self-esteem. Even deliberately doing something to value yourself for, so that you can write it down in your notebook, is valuable and therapeutic, so please do that.

It could be so nurturing that you may also get a warm glow and pleasure from actually deliberately doing something that you value yourself for.

Make sure that when you have written down the three things that you value yourself for on a particular day, then write down 'And I love and appreciate myself'. Read that out also.

You may happily write this phrase and read it and start to experience the benefit. Or, you might resist and say something like: 'I don't believe this, I don't actually love and appreciate myself, why should I write it down? It isn't true.'

My reply to that is: 'Please do it anyway.' Write down, 'And I love and appreciate myself'. Gradually you will start to feel the benefits of doing this. Again, the part of you that needs to hear this phrase won't question it and will believe you, and this is what we need to happen for you.

Quite soon you will gradually feel better in terms of your self-worth and self-esteem.

'Gradually you will start to feel the benefits.'

Eventually you will begin to enjoy completing the exercise and doing small things, and even greater things, that you can value yourself for. This can be an exercise that runs through your journey towards positive change and improve how you feel about yourself.

Learning how to value yourself until it becomes second-nature to you is very important. It will enable you to have much greater confidence in yourself, have a greater sense of self-worth and help to lift any depression. You will be able to manage situations with which you have previously had difficulty.

A client story 1 – Nathan

Nathan sought counseling after he'd suffered a sudden irretrievable breakdown of his marriage. His wife had moved out and had begun a relationship with another man. His wife had a history of being verbally abusive towards Nathan and over a period of time this had worn him down, resulting in him having a poor opinion of himself and feeling that he couldn't cope. He was left caring for his two children, selling the family home and sorting out finances. He was not able to go to his job and, doubting his abilities, felt incapable of sorting his life out. He was knocked sideways.

During counseling I encouraged Nathan to begin to do the Valuing Exercise. He found it a little difficult at the beginning, but was soon able to fully engage with it. Gradually he began to value the things that he was able to achieve for himself and his children. For example he made sure that he made healthy meals and got sufficient sleep. He showered each day and cleaned his teeth (these everyday occurrences had slipped in his initial distress). He tidied himself up, and started to wear smarter clothes. He valued that fact that he kept in touch with the relevant people at work and attended meetings with his solicitor.

He valued the ways in which he was showing that he valued himself.

Over a few weeks Nathan gradually began to feel better and was happy with the way he was able to manage his life. He felt much more positive about his future and could see his way ahead. He mentioned that the Valuing Exercise had been a vital part in his progress, and that it was something that he intended to continue doing, even when his counseling sessions had ended.

Valuing yourself in the workplace

To survive in a stressful workplace you have to value yourself. Sometimes people do not consider themselves sufficient in certain situations. They don't have a high enough opinion of themselves, always put other people first and help them instead of looking after themselves. Eventually they may run out of steam and become exhausted.

Some people feel quite uncomfortable about putting themselves first and feel that it is selfish to do so. If this applies to you it is likely to be because of the way you were conditioned as a child to please others.

Valuing yourself increases your self-esteem and self-worth and helps you to develop an inner resilience. This helps to ensure that you do not allow yourself to be taken advantage of in the workplace and end up doing more and more until you are working beyond your remit, working too many hours and feeling out of control.

To survive in the workplace, it is OK for you to look after yourself and make sure that you keep to the boundaries of your job and stick to your job description. Take your breaks and your lunch times. Be assertive and persistent in maintaining the boundaries of your job. As you do this, write down each step that you take in your valuing notebook. Value the steps that you have taken to value yourself.

'It is OK for you to be at the center of your own life.'

People who do not value themselves often do not see themselves at the centre of their own lives. In the process of doing the Valuing Exercise over time, you will begin to realise that it is OK for you to be at the center of your own life, and to be so without feeling guilty. By this I mean that it is OK to do what is right for you, in order to take care of yourself.

The words 'I love and appreciate myself' can have an impact on how you feel about yourself and affect your attitude and your behavior towards yourself.

Are you a person who feels uncomfortable about putting yourself first? The result is that you may end up putting yourself last. Sometimes it is out of our awareness that we are doing this. Even though I am aware of this kind of thing, I've been prone to this myself in the past. For example, I've caught myself serving food for the family and giving myself the smallest bit, or the untidy cut-off from the end of an item of food. Now I make sure that I give myself a decent piece or portion of whatever it is that I am serving.

If you 'do' for others and not so much for yourself, eventually you could become jaded and worn-out and 'run out of steam'. To use the analogy of a pack of cards, instead of putting yourself at the bottom of the pack of cards, try putting yourself half way up the pack of cards, or even at the top occasionally. Doing this you will begin to feel better about yourself, and more energised and happier.

A client story 2 – Jane

Jane came to me for counseling and was off work with stress. Jane felt that her stress was largely due to the demands put on her at work, which in part was the case. She worked as an administrator in a hospital setting, in an office with other people doing similar roles. Being able to talk in her counseling sessions helped to begin to alleviate her distress. Also, she found the Breathing and Calming Exercise that I gave her very helpful and she felt less anxious and panicky, more relaxed and calm. (See the Free Gift PDF 'Simple Breathing and Calming Method').

Jane thought that the work place had to change until I gently pointed out to her that it was herself that would need to change. Jane began to realise that she had been missing her breaks and curtailing her lunch time. She had been helping her colleagues out to such an extent that she'd ended up working more hours than she was paid for. Jane said that, unlike herself, her colleagues had young children to collect and needed to get away from work on time. Jane had been putting herself at the 'bottom of the pile' and not taking herself into consideration and valuing herself. She felt out of control. I asked her to start doing the Valuing Exercise.

Through doing the Valuing Exercise Jane's self-esteem began to improve and she gradually felt ready to go back to work. When back at work she made sure that she took her breaks and the lunchtime period that she was entitled to. She left work on time, keeping to the hours that she was contracted to work. As a result, she felt much calmer and happier at work. Jane said that she wanted to continue with the Valuing Exercise to maintain progress and improve her self-esteem further.

People often hopelessly confuse the idea of self-love with being selfish. It is good to learn to love yourself and to take care of yourself. Think of yourself like a garden. A garden has to be tended in order to flourish and bloom. Likewise, take care of yourself and nourish yourself so that you continue to feel good. Self-love is perfectly OK. It is OK to love yourself.

'Self-love is perfectly OK. It is OK to love yourself.'

Summary

- Do the Valuing Exercise every day.
- Love and appreciate yourself.
- Valuing yourself will improve your self-esteem.

2

Recognize your daily achievements

"Act as if what you do makes a difference. It does."

—*William James*

Continue to do the Valuing Exercise daily and make it a priority to do so. Become accustomed to doing it so that it becomes a good lifestyle habit. You will be astounded with the benefits that you will experience.

Today a client told me that he was really enjoying doing the exercise and that it often brought a smile to his face. The fact that he was completing the daily Valuing Exercise had resulted in him taking action and doing certain things, from which he had really felt the benefit.

'You will be astounded with the benefits.'

He was definitely beginning to feel better as a result of doing the Valuing Exercise.

Sometimes people forget to write something down and remember it days later and then write it down. It is OK to do this.

You may wish to download an app on your smart phone which encourages you and reminds you to do the exercise each day. A good app example is HabitBull. This app can be used for a variety of purposes and can help you to build positive habits (and break bad habits). In addition to reminding you to do the daily Valuing Exercise, the app allows you to tick it off once you have done it. This creates a 'streak' or 'chain' day after day that you will most likely be reluctant to break. This encourages you to continue with the Valuing Exercise.

Generally, people forget to value themselves and are more focused on what they do for others, valuing what they do for others instead of what they do for themselves. Ultimately a person may wear themselves out. (This point is worth repeating.)

They have forgotten how to really look after themselves in a physical, emotional and psychological way. They start to realize that they need to factor themselves more into their own lives. Doing the Valuing Exercise helps them to begin to do this. Some examples of physical actions they may take to value themselves are:

- Having 'me' time.

- Rest periods.

- Meeting friends for a coffee.

- Window shopping.

- Reading.

- Going out for walks, especially in nature.

These activities will help the person mentally and emotionally and may help you. If you are already doing this, well done - jot it down in your valuing notebook.

It is all too easy to lack awareness about our daily achievements. We have been so busy, in this busy world, and time has gone so fast, that we do not realize what we have achieved in the course of a day or part of a day.

How many times have you said: 'I've done nothing today'? Or 'I haven't done much today'? I know that I have! This can be undermining and soul-destroying.

It can be incredibly helpful to just stop, think about and list what you have done so far during this day.

You could write this in your valuing notebook.

What have you done today so far? What jobs, errands, activities have you undertaken?

Be aware of what each activity entails. Take the example of making a meal:

- What ingredient shopping was needed?
- What preparation did you need to do?
- What was entailed in the preparation?
- How long did it take?
- Factor in the clearing up from the preparation.
- Factor in the washing up after the meal.

Because many of the things you do during a day are routine, or even mundane and automatic, you may tend not to notice them and recognize what you have achieved.

The Valuing Exercise can be a real eye opener and a boost to your sense of achievement, and ultimately your self-esteem and self-worth.

> *'The Valuing Exercise can be a real eye-opener.'*

Write down how you feel now, after recognizing your achievements. I often work with clients to enable them to recognize their own abilities. They may lack confidence and not appreciate and see how capable they really are. In a challenging situation they may be worried and anxious about what might happen next and whether they will be able to manage the situation. There is nothing worse than 'not knowing' and a fear of the unknown.

This can create great anxiety in some people and depression.

Very often the person hasn't recognized or realized that they have in the past already dealt with and managed, challenging situations.

Recognizing their achievements can be reassuring to the person; they feel more settled and confident about managing the unknowns that may happen in the future.

Your valuing notebook can provide you with similar reassurance. If you read your previous entries you will more than likely gain reassurance from reminding yourself of some of your achievements.

In the process of doing the Valuing Exercise over time, you may begin to realize that it is OK for you to be at the centre of your own life and without feeling guilty.

Summary

- Recognize your daily achievements.

- Write them down in your notebook and then write down how you feel.

3

Keep a personal journal – Delight in your progress

"What lies behind us and what lies before us are tiny matters compared to what lies within us."

—Ralph Waldo Emerson

KEEP A PERSONAL JOURNAL

In the previous chapters I encouraged you to begin to do the Valuing Exercise and to have a special notebook for that purpose. Developing that exercise further, you may wish to keep a daily personal journal. With many people this occurs quite naturally as a result of completing the daily Valuing Exercise. They want to write more and expand on what they have valued themselves for. They also wish to record what they have achieved that day and recognize and record their progress and how the Valuing Exercise has made a difference to them.

'You may be amazed at what you have achieved.'

Very often we do not appreciate how much we have achieved in the day. This may be because we are just 'getting on with it' as the time passes, or because we do not actually appreciate and value our own achievements. You may be amazed at what you have achieved.

How do you feel doing the Valuing Exercise?

On a day-to-day basis you will be writing down your three things that you value yourself for. You may notice how you feel and what you are thinking as you do this – write this down too.

- What effect did the action that you valued yourself for have on you?

- How do you feel as a result?

- How did this affect your mood?

- What else did you do today?

If you wish, make extra notes every day. What benefits are you noticing from doing the Valuing Exercise?

In committing to and completing the daily Valuing Exercise, you are entering a process which ultimately will enable you to feel better about yourself.

Affirmations

Affirmations are positive statements that can help you to challenge and overcome self-sabotaging and negative thoughts.

Fill your journal with affirmations about loving and appreciating yourself. Write down a different affirmation each day. You could do this on a smart phone, or other digital device, but the act of physically writing in a notebook or journal is shown to be more effective and therapeutic. Here are some affirmations to start you off.

I am proud of myself and all that I have accomplished.

I love myself unconditionally and accept myself as I am.

I acknowledge my own self worth and my confidence is soaring.

I shall lovingly accept myself as I am right now.

I am creating a beautiful life.

My self esteem is growing day by day.

I believe in my abilities.

You can also devise your own affirmations and/or search for them on the Internet.

Whenever you feel self-doubt coming on, simply refer to your journal. Read some of your daily notes and notice your progress.

Benefits of journaling

Studies have shown that:

- People who journal experience better moods.
- Journaling helps to reduce stress.
- Regular journaling is an effective tool to fight depression and anxiety.
- People who journal don't get sick as often.

- Journaling can even help people to fight disease.
- Healing from medical procedures occurs faster in people who journal, as opposed to those who don't.

In terms of self-help, there are few things quite so effective at changing your life as journaling.

> *'There are few things quite so effective at changing your life as journaling.'*

Write down all your achievements that you can remember. Think back as far as you can. Don't limit yourself. If you had achievements in high school or college, put those down as well. This action will help to show you everything that you have achieved. It will give you confidence in your ability to accomplish anything you set your mind to.

The way to ensure that journaling works for you is to do it long-term. Long-term journaling gives you more insight into your life, because you'll be able to look at the past and the present. It will also increase your self awareness. You'll need to journal daily to make it a habit. Here are a few tips for making journaling part of your daily routine:

- Make it easy. Generally it is easier to use a notebook and paper than a computer. Have your notebook readily available in your bag or on your bedside table.

- Find a time that works for you. The best times to do it are early morning, first thing, or last thing before you go to bed: whatever is best for you.

- Find time and space for yourself and make yourself comfortable. It will be easier to get into the right frame of mind.

- You could choose a particular type of journal. Some people prefer to use a specific style or format of journaling, like bullet journaling, prayer journaling or project journaling.

- Certain journals have prompts in them, or sentence starters. These are available online.

- Reward yourself when you have been journaling for a length of time, such as one month. Take time to read what you have written.

Summary

- Keep a personal journal.

- Write down how you feel in your personal journal.

- Look for affirmations online or devise your own.

- Write down your affirmations.

4

Listen to your self-talk: the chatter inside your head

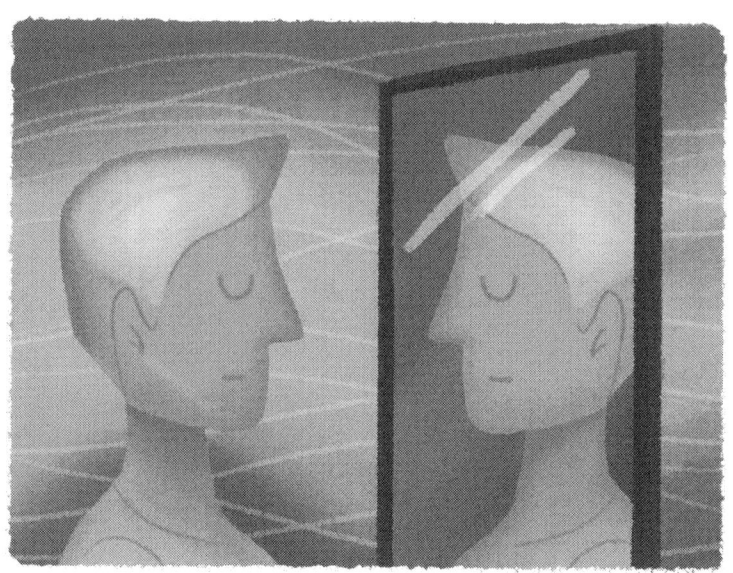

"Be who you are and say what you feel, because those who mind don't matter and those who matter don't mind."

—Dr. Seuss

LISTEN TO YOUR SELF-TALK

Very often people can be quite unaware of the quality of their thought processes, especially as to how negative or positive their thoughts are. We often have a dialogue going on inside our heads, a conversation or chatter.

Whichever they are, positive or negative, your thoughts will have a significant impact on how you feel. As well as your thoughts affecting how you feel, they may well affect what happens and what you do. If you tend to think negatively much of the time, then this could result in you feeling low and depressed and having feelings of poor self-worth and poor self-esteem. It could also lead to you going into a downward spiral. You really don't need this. The reverse is true. If you tend to think in a more positive way, then you are much more likely to feel good and have a good self-esteem and self-worth.

> *'Whichever they are, positive or negative, your thoughts will have a significant impact on how you feel.'*

Whichever way you choose to think becomes a self-fulfilling prophecy.

To begin to address any negative chatter, start by paying attention to the things that you say when speaking to someone else. In this scenario you will be speaking out loud: you will hear yourself and it'll be easy to notice yourself talking negatively.

Some examples are:

- When asked how they are, some people might say: 'I'm not so bad'. A positive reply would be: 'I'm ok', or 'I'm doing well', or 'I'm good thank you'.

- When asked how they are, some people might say: 'I can't complain'. A positive reply would be: 'I am doing well', or 'I'm feeling well, thanks'.

From this exercise you can become much more aware of the chatter inside your head. Identify the negative thought and ask yourself: 'What would I be thinking right now if I were to think more positively?' Turn the negative thought into a positive thought.

Some examples of negative thoughts:

- 'Things always go wrong for me' is negative. 'Usually things go OK for me' is positive.

- 'I haven't done much today' is negative. Turn it into what you have done and you'll immediately feel better. It is positive to say instead: 'I've done some food shopping, changed the cat litter box, put the washing out to dry, taken the washing in off the line and folded it, and tidied the lounge.'

- 'I'm silly for spilling my drink' is negative. Instead, 'Oh that was a silly thing to do' is positive and is separating you from your behavior.

- 'I've never been successful' is negative, whilst 'I have had some successes' is positive.

- 'I'm an idiot' is obviously negative, whilst 'I am a good person' is positive.

How do you feel now that you have done that? Notice how different you feel by thinking more positively.

Write this down in your valuing notebook. Value yourself for thinking in a positive way.

You will feel happier if you can adopt a more positive way of thinking.

You'll also feel happier as a result of valuing yourself for thinking positively. You will feel happier as you progress with the Valuing Exercise and begin to think and behave in a way that shows that you value yourself.

'You will feel happier as you progress with the Valuing Exercise.'

Avoid being hard on yourself if you slip up. It is OK to be kind to yourself.

The power of positivity

Optimism can be powerful enough to turn thoughts and feelings around. Even if a situation seems impossible to change, being optimistic can make a difference. Optimists are able to create an alternate world where things work for them and fall into place.

> **Oxford Dictionary Definition**
>
> *Positivity* – The practice of being or tendency to be positive or optimistic in attitude.

Due to their positive disposition, optimists can develop resistance to depression. They can become more resilient, happier and more successful.

I've observed, as you probably have also, various sports people who have improved their mindset over time, from negative to positive. In past interviews I've noticed how negative they were about their abilities, fitness, etc. and how they rehearsed negative outcomes. The result being that they did not achieve the results that they were capable of. Over time, perhaps after they have acquired a new coach or psychologist to work with them, I've noticed their attitude become more positive: consequently their results have improved immensely.

Developing a positive attitude

It is not always easy to stay positive. The world is filled with a lot of negativity, and if you allow yourself to be submerged in it, then it could begin to affect you. Avoid negativity when you can, for example, don't watch news 'on loop'.

Do as much as you can to surround yourself with positive energy so that you can develop a positive attitude. Immerse yourself with positive energy, either through the people who you are with or the situations that you permit yourself to be a part of.

If you are with people who are negative, they may well bring you down. Associate with people who are positive, so that you can share in their optimism. Let their optimism rub off on you.

'Embrace positivity and feel great.'

Learn to look at things from a different perspective. If something negative comes your way, see if you can turn it into something positive. Look at it from a different angle, and maybe you will see a silver lining.

It is OK to avoid becoming a victim to negativity.

Embrace positivity and feel great.

Summary

- Listen to your self-talk.
- Optimism can be powerful enough to turn things around.

Value You

- Surround yourself with positive energy and positive people.

5

Find the hero inside yourself: Value and recognize your self-worth

"If you are still looking for that one person who will change your life, take a look in the mirror."

—*Roman Price*

Many of us, possibly you included, have attributes that we have 'lost' or forgotten about, and this can lead to losing our confidence and doubting our ability to do certain things. We may feel lost and inadequate in some way.

Perhaps you:

- Have got out of the habit of doing something you used to do.

- Have relied on someone too heavily to do certain things for you that you could have done for yourself, and perhaps that person is no longer around through bereavement or separation.

- Have certain skills that have 'gone out of focus' due to a recent stressful time.

- Have had a lack of time, been overwhelmed and/or over-worked so that certain things have dropped out of your daily life.

- Life has passed you by.

    ...and so on.

You could add your thoughts and ideas to the list above.

Doing the daily Valuing Exercise, keeping a personal journal and recognizing your daily achievements can help greatly with these matters. Listening to your self-talk is also vital, as we discussed in the previous chapter. Maintaining a positive mindset and internal dialogue, rather than dragging yourself down with negative self-talk, can be most beneficial.

When you feel more confident in yourself it could be time to set some small goals to enable you to tap into and use your skills and attributes. In fact, find the hero inside yourself.

At this point I'd like to refer you to 'Search for the Hero' by M People and sung by Heather Small.

For many years I ran Counseling Skills courses and I included this song in the programme for students to discuss. They loved it. It enabled them to appreciate the resources they had within themselves, and that in turn gave them an inner confidence and reassurance.

You can listen to the original version here:

https://bit.ly/valueyou1

and read the lyrics here:

https://bit.ly/valueyou2

The song is meaningful to many people and soulful. It is worth listening to. Pick out the lyrics which resonate with you. What do the lyrics mean to you?

Here are some of them:

'You've got to search for the hero inside yourself
Search for the secrets you hide
Search for the hero inside yourself
Until you find the key to your life.'

These lyrics sum up what we have been talking about in this book, especially in this current chapter.

What do they mean to you? Write down in your notebook or journal what thoughts and feelings you have about the lyrics.

'Because you and only you alone
Can build a bridge across the stream.'

You are the one who knows, at some level, what skills and attributes you have inside you. These skills could be ones that you learned as an adult. Some may have been learned during your childhood, possibly by watching your mother or father do something.

As an adult you are responsible for building the bridge across the stream. And you need to build the bridge across the stream in order to reach and access your skills and attributes, and get to where you want to be in your life.

However sometimes some people need help to build the bridge across the stream. We cannot always do things all by ourselves. It is OK to ask for help from a friend, relative, or health professional such as a counselor.

'Do whatever you feel is necessary to find the hero inside yourself.'

Do whatever you feel is necessary to find the hero inside yourself.' *And that's why, you should keep on aiming high Just seek yourself and you will shine.'*

You really can feel better and have a good sense of self-worth and self-esteem. Listening to 'Search for the Hero' will inspire you and encourage you.

Confidence boost

Here are some tips on how to feel better and more confident:

- Do something that you love. You will feel better if you do that. No matter how sad or how lonely you feel now, if you do something that you love you will feel some element of relief. Make some notes in your notebook or journal.

- Never compare yourself with others. You are an individual and unique. You are OK as you are.

- Think positively and do something positive. Don't dwell on negative thoughts because it can lead you into negative actions. If you constantly think that you are worthless, you will eventually do something that will prove that you are worthless. It is important for you to **think** positively and **do** something positive in order to boost your self-confidence. If you can accompany your positive thoughts with positive action you will achieve great results and feel fantastic.

- Change your posture and the way you walk. My clients would tell you that I like to encourage people to be aware of and change their posture in certain situations.

The posture of a confident person is different to that of a person lacking in confidence. A confident person will walk upright, reflecting their confidence. A less confident person will tend to walk with a slumped posture.

If you change your posture, and the way you walk, you will instantly feel different. This is all about body language: by changing your body language you can change how you feel.

When I was supply teaching 11-16 year old students, I kept this in mind. Some students think that they can take advantage of a supply teacher because they think that the teacher is not 'up to speed' with the policies and workings of the school. So, even though I felt a little nervous walking into a class of 25 students, I made sure that I walked into the classroom in an upright manner, with purpose and engaging eye contact with them. I am sure that this enabled me to have greater control of the class than if I had walked in looking at the floor and seeming nervous.

Congratulate yourself when you do good things, however small, whether it is for you or someone else. Make sure that you recognize and acknowledge the smaller things. They do count and are as important as the larger things. Please make sure that you jot them down in your valuing book or journal.

More tips to help you feel great about yourself

- Remind yourself of your accomplishments.

- Accept compliments graciously. Many people do not know how to accept compliments, largely because, as children, we tended to be told what we had done wrong and what not to do, rather than what we had done well and what to do. Some people are uncomfortable with compliments and will tend to push them away and make some counter-comment, such as 'Oh it's nothing' or 'I bought it in a charity shop'. Does that sound familiar to you? Make sure that you embrace compliments. If someone compliments you about your work, or someone tells you that you are look nice, smile, and thank them. Let the compliment soak in: embody it, so that you feel the benefit.

'Let the compliment soak in: embody it.'

- Believe in your abilities. Have faith in yourself. Believe that you can achieve things. You may like to enrol on a course. Knowledge can boost your confidence.

Summary

- Search for the hero inside yourself.

- Value and recognize your self-worth.

- Remember the tips that help you to feel more confident about yourself.

6

Be kind to yourself and build your self-esteem

"Go above and beyond for yourself! You do it for family, friends, and colleagues, but don't forget about YOU. It's important to include yourself. You are worthy of your own kindness too!"

—*Stephanie Lahart*

BE KIND TO YOURSELF

People can be their own worst critic and far too ready to put themselves down, blame themselves, or turn anger in on themselves. This is self-destructive and self-harming and can ultimately lead to depression.

Do you have a tendency to do this?

This can become a self-perpetuating vicious circle, resulting in a lack of confidence, poor self-worth and poor self-esteem, even to the extent of hating yourself in some cases.

A VICIOUS CIRCLE

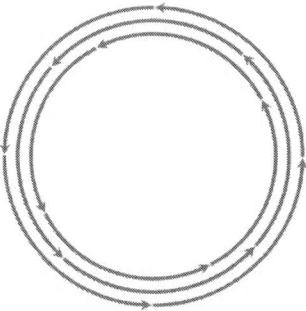

One way of breaking this vicious circle and finding a way off it, is to be **kind to yourself**.

This may be easier said than done for some people. A good way to do this is to do the Valuing Exercise that we covered in Chapter 1.

How can you be kinder to yourself?

Listen to your self-talk and if you catch yourself being unkind to yourself, ask:

- How do I feel right now?
- What would I be thinking right now if I was being kind to myself?
- What could I say or do, right now, to be kind to myself?

Say to yourself in a kind, gentle tone of voice: 'I'm OK'. 'It is OK to be kind to myself'.

Or say to yourself: 'What can I do to be kind to myself? Go for a walk, make myself a cup of tea, buy myself some flowers, have a nice relaxing bath?'

- How do I feel as a result of being kind to myself?

Having done some of the above examples you can then complete your Valuing Exercise for the day. In doing so you are valuing yourself and reinforcing the positive.

Continue writing in your personal journal - derive the benefits that can be achieved from doing that.

Revisit 'Find the Hero Inside Yourself' - Chapter 5.

Keeping all these steps in focus and putting them into action will enable you to break the vicious circle.

BREAKING THE VICIOUS CIRCLE

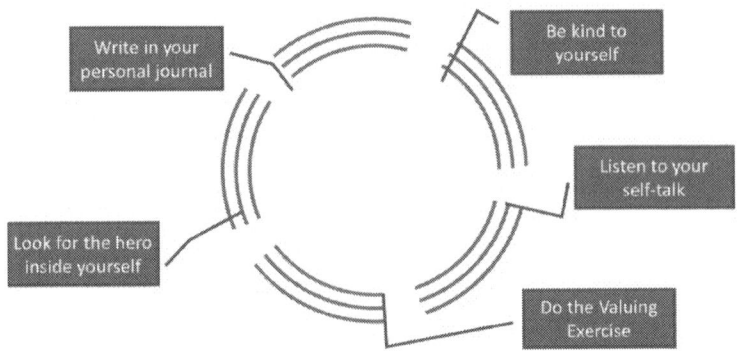

Through the process of doing the Valuing Exercise, over time, you will begin to like and love yourself. The phrase, 'love yourself' is often very misunderstood and mistaken for being selfish. Self-love and being selfish are very different.

Self-love enables a person to feel good about themselves and more able to interact and be with other people, or to help other people. A person who behaves in a selfish way feels less good about themselves and has less to offer or give to others.

Building your self-esteem

Through doing the Valuing Exercise and other activities suggested in this book you will learn to love yourself and build your self-esteem.

The important thing is to begin and to start small, with realistic goals. Lots of small goals collectively are bigger than one big goal. Over time they will have a cumulative effect on how well you feel.

In a nutshell, you will begin to feel different and know that there is something different within you.

You will start to have the confidence to access the resources that have been within you all the time.

'The important thing is to begin and to start small, with realistic goals.'

It is okay to pay attention to your own needs and wants.

Value You

You are important too. You deserve some attention. Learn to pamper and be kind to yourself.

Summary

- Be kind to yourself and build your self-esteem.
- Take steps to break the vicious circle.
- Start with small steps and with realistic goals.

7

Get to 'I'm OK and you're OK': Bringing it all together

"If you have the ability to love, love yourself."

— *Charles Bukowski*

It may well be, that when you started reading this book, you were coming from a place of 'You're OK, I'm not OK'. Hopefully the process that you have been through whilst following the ideas in this book has enabled you to start getting to a position of 'I'm OK, you're OK' more often.

You were born perfectly OK. However, during early childhood, this position is likely to have changed due to your subjective perceptions of the experiences of your environment.

As small children we are totally reliant on our parents and significant others for nurture, food and being looked after and kept safe. On observing a child, we can see how dependant he or she is on the adults around him/her.

'You were born perfectly OK.'

Even in the case of good parenting, a child will experience conflicting thoughts and feelings. The way the child deals with this is to make the decision 'You're OK, I'm not OK'.

The ideas above are from the established model of therapy which is called Transactional Analysis (TA). TA is the study of human behaviour and how humans interrelate with each other.

As we go through life it is possible to assess and change these early decisions. Teenagers often rebel and, in doing so, sometimes make new decisions about themselves.

Significant life events as an adult can also alter the way we think about ourselves. However, many of us still think about ourselves in the 'You're OK, - I'm not OK' position.

In reading this book and committing yourself to the Valuing Exercise in Chapter 1, and the concepts in the other chapters, you will be well on your way to 'You're OK, I'm OK' and feeling so much better, with increased self-worth and self-esteem. This will make a big impact on many areas of your life, for example your relationships with other people, your work, and your career.

Summary

- Assess and work on changing those early decisions that you made about yourself when you were a child.

- Work towards getting to 'You're OK, I'm OK'.

My Message to You

I encourage you to trust the process of following and working on the concepts covered in this book, *Value You*.

The concepts are simple but profound in their effectiveness.

Take action now.

In Appendix 1, I share comments that I have received from grateful clients over the years, with particular reference to the Valuing Exercise.

Appendix 1

Client comments on the Valuing Exercise

Here are some comments and feedback that I have received from clients about their experience of doing the Valuing Exercise.

'The Valuing Exercise has really helped me to help myself.'

'Before I do things I now ask myself if I am valuing myself in doing these things.'

'I have found that I am now being kinder to myself.'

'The Valuing Exercise enabled me to have a more positive mindset and outlook.'

'The Valuing Exercise has helped me a lot. I have stepped back and looked at what I am doing.'

'I have regained positivity and confidence.'

'I want to continue to make valuing myself part of my daily activities.'

'The Valuing Exercise has helped me to regain appropriate control over my life and I have gained so much confidence.'

'The Valuing Exercise has helped me to get through my difficulties, because I kept the idea of valuing myself in my mind.'

'The Valuing Exercise has helped me such a lot. I am finding it easier to do now and I feel good about myself. I feel of value and worth something.'

I feel sure that in a little while you too could be experiencing some of the benefits that these people have expressed. Feel free to contact me to let me know.

Appendix 2

Valuing Exercise form

I value myself for

....

....

I value myself for

....

....

I value myself for

....

....

And I love and appreciate myself.

Remember your free gift

As a "thank you" for obtaining this book, I'd like to give you a free gift: a PDF called *Simple Breathing and Calming Method*. It is worth its weight in gold.

Here's the link: www.selfhealsystems.com/free

I hope that you find this helpful.

Work with me

I've worked with clients face-to-face, over the phone and on video calls for more than 25 years.

Contact me if you are interested in working with me – anne@selfhealsystems.com.

One final thing...

I would really appreciate it if you would review my book on Amazon.

Also, you can drop me a line or ask me questions by emailing me at anne@selfhealsystems.com.

Index

Achievements, 41, 45, 47, 48, 49, 53, 57, 74

Affirmations, 55, 59

Compliments, 80, 81

Confidence, 17, 30, 32, 47, 55, 57, 73, 77, 78, 79, 81, 85, 89, 99

Depression, 23, 24, 25, 32, 48, 56, 67, 85

Examples, 27, 28, 45, 87

HabitBull, 44

Heather Small, 74, 75

Hero, 74, 77, 87

I'm OK, You're OK, 91, 93, 94, 95

Journal, 51, 53, 55, 56, 57, 58, 59, 74, 76, 78, 80, 87

Journaling, 56, 57, 58, 59

  tips for, 58

M People, 74

Making a meal, 46

Optimism, 67, 69

Positive attitude, 68

  developing, 68

Positivity

  power of, 67

Progress, 2, 24, 53, 56, 66
Search for the Hero Inside Yourself, 74, 77
Self-esteem, 17, 18, 23, 24, 31, 34, 47, 63, 77, 83, 85, 89, 90, 95
Self-fulfilling prophecy, 64
Self-love, 39, 88
Self-talk, 61, 69, 74, 86
Self-worth, 18, 23, 24, 30, 31, 32, 34, 47, 63, 77, 82, 85, 95

Stress, 56
Teenagers, 94
Transactional Analysis, 15, 94
Unknown
fear of, 47
Valuing Exercise, 43, 47, 54, 74, 86, 87, 88, 89, 94, 99
Valuing yourself, 21, 26, 27, 28, 29, 30, 31, 32, 34, 35, 39, 54, 66, 87
Workplace, 24, 34, 35
Written exercise, 25

Printed in Poland
by Amazon Fulfillment
Poland Sp. z o.o., Wrocław